The Language of Loss

Haiku & Tanka Conversations

Debbie Strange

Cover and interior design by Daniel Krawiec

ISBN 978-1-7333671-2-7

Sable Books
sablebooks.org

in memory of
Mike, Kelly, Elizabeth, and Curtis Strange
the missing branch
of our family tree

Contents

"Your absence has gone through me
Like thread through a needle.
Everything I do is stitched with its color."

— W.S. Merwin

rainbows
spin from the crest
of a wave . . .
I wish we'd had more
time to say goodbye

feathers
on the empty beach
I write his name

a star tortoise
carries the universe
on its back . . .
are we slowly moving
away from each other

dark matter
we never plan
to be alone

chain lightning
crawls across the sky . . .
purple flashes
unlock her memory
of childhood bruises

dense fog
the softened beacon
of an ambulance

ancient graves
sink into marshland . . .
the long bones
of our ancestors
wandering, still

hollyhocks
our parents grow smaller
every year

I measure
my horse at his withers . . .
these hands
know how to gentle
everything but you

chiaroscuro
I let go of the need
to appease

ghost-light
above the coulee
an antelope
lies down beside
my sister

crow moon . . .
it would have been
her birthday

an orca
held her dead calf
afloat for weeks . . .
they tell me I should
be over it by now

stillborn . . .
I long to grow flowers
instead of stones

a yellow leaf
lets go of the tree . . .
she held on
long past the time
for surrender

the whistle
of a wood duck . . .
her last breath

a necklace
of sea foam traces
the bay's curve
I pine for this amity
between earth and water

loneliness
the holes we fill
with something else

small embers
of rose hips in snow . . .
the look
in mother's vacant eyes
so hard to define

our names
escape her
fireflies

we offer her
to the warm earth
in a silence
more eloquent than any
language of loss

gone too soon
sakura blossoms
my old friends

overnight,
filaments of hair ice
grow longer . . .
how tenuous these threads
that bind us to each other

emergency flares
above us the crackle
of northern lights

afterthoughts
blacker than our last
conversation . . .
the skeletal remains
of old-growth forests

change of life
the planet and I
heating up

a smudge
of blackbirds swirling
into evening . . .
how fluid the shape
of this sorrow

diurnal tides
the ebb and flow
of grief

scented drifts
of cottonwood fluff
line every street . . .
he might not make it
through the winter

dad's books . . .
the thumbprints of who
he used to be

every forest
embraces its shadows
but mine
are too dark and deep
for such intimacy

split chrysalis
all the ways we learn
to become small

uncertainty
seeps through the fog . . .
we can't find
our footing on this bridge
already crossed

stone cairns
a faded cap drifts
downriver

a car filled
with catcalling men
follows me ...
I long to walk alone
in the sweet evening air

city sirens
the wolves that used to
sing us home

wavering veils
of snow geese in transit
remind me
of the way life comes
together . . . falls apart

heirlooms
the time we meant
to make

a bird's nest
bound with spidersilk . . .
nothing
to hold us together
after the young had flown

the *yink* and *yank*
of white-breasted nuthatches
we no longer speak

we are kin
to birds of passage
wintering
in far-flung places,
never quite at home

windblown seeds
refugees try to cross
the border

farm auction . . .
we have nothing
left to lose
except these thistles
rooted in our hearts

empty nest
on the *for sale* sign
mourning doves

crafted with love,
this table you made
from ash trees
planted for the children
we never had

deep canyon
our prayers sink
to the bottom

hares boxing
in the flush of dawn . . .
it seems
impossible to defeat
an opponent I can't see

bone density . . .
the broken stems
of sunflowers

the gleam
of copper birches
in sunlight . . .
she wears her wounds
with gravitas

haloed moon . . .
an aureole tattoo where
her breast was

for a moment,
two waterspouts dance
across the lake . . .
I still feel your hand
on the small of my back

the blue hour . . .
you slipped away
without a sound

the borrowed
identities of frogs
and butterflies ...
sometimes she cannot
recognize my face

thin ice
the broken mosaic
of her memory

wisps of clouds
hover across the horizon
if only they were
doves offering branches
of peace to this world

gulls hunched
along the shoreline
more bad news

my neighbour,
evicted while in rehab . . .
a dumpster
overflows with the dregs
of his woebegone life

homeless
wet leaves seal the holes
in his boots

thirty-five
types of snowflakes . . .
no one told me
that they would
all taste the same

cabbage whites
shreds of the letter
I never sent

we avoid
the place in which
they found you
but our thoughts
often take us there

a *cold case*
our hope lingers
ten winters

bind my body
with spanworm silk
lay me down
in a shaded garden
until I turn to earth

dying moth . . .
not everyone makes it
to the light

Publication Credits

My sincere thanks to the editors of the following publications in which these poems first appeared:

Atlas Poetica : A Journal of World Tanka
Australian Haiku Society
Bleached Butterfly Magazine
Blithe Spirit : Journal of the British Haiku Society
Bottle Rockets : A Collection of Short Verse
Cattails : Journal of the United Haiku and Tanka Society
Chrysanthemum : Magazine for Modern Poetic Forms in the Tradition of
        Japanese Short Poetry
Creatrix : Poetry and Haiku Journal
Ephemerae
Failed Haiku : A Journal of English Senryū
#FemkuMag : An E-zine of Womxn's Haiku
Frameless Sky : A Japanese Short-Form Poetry Video Journal
Frogpond : The Journal of the Haiku Society of America
Gnarled Oak : An Online Literary Journal
GUSTS : Contemporary Tanka
Human/Kind Journal
Incense Dreams Journal
Lyrical Passion Poetry E-zine
Mariposa
Modern Haiku : An Independent Journal of Haiku and Haiku Studies
Moonbathing : A Journal of Women's Tanka
Of Love and War and the Life In Between : Tanka Society of America
        Members' Anthology, 2018
On Down the Road : Haiku Society of America Members' Anthology, 2017
Presence
Red Lights
Ribbons : Tanka Society of America Journal
Scryptic : Magazine of Alternative Art
Seedpods : E-newsletter of the United Haiku and Tanka Society
Shamrock : Haiku Journal of the Irish Haiku Society
Skylark Tanka Journal
The Bamboo Hut : A Journal of English Language Tanshi
Under the Bashō
Unsealing Our Secrets : A Short Poem Anthology About Sexual Abuse, 2018
Wordless : Haiku Canada — 40 Years of Haiku, 2017

Award Credits (in order of appearance)

"a star tortoise" – 2nd Place, 2018 San Francisco Int'l Competition for Haiku, Senryū and Tanka

"the whistle" – Honourable Mention, 2015 Betty Drevniok Award

"small embers" – 3rd Place, 2018 San Francisco Int'l Competition for Haiku, Senryū and Tanka

"gone too soon" – Sakura Award, 2015 Vancouver Cherry Blossom Festival Haiku Invitational

"a smudge" – 2nd Place, 2018 Fleeting Words Tanka Competition

"split chrysalis" – Museum of Haiku Literature Award, Blithe Spirit 26.1, 2016

"stone cairns" – 1st Place, 2015 Harold G. Henderson Award for Best Unpublished Haiku

"city sirens" – Runner-up, 2019 Shamrock Haiku Journal Readers' Choice Awards

"empty nest" – Selected Haiku, 2015 Yamadera Bashō Memorial Museum Haiku Contest

"crafted with love" – Honourable Mention, 2019 World Tanka Contest

Acknowledgements

I offer my gratitude to Roberta Beary, judge of the 2019 Sable Books Haiku Book Contest for Women, for her sensitive and insightful reading of *The Language of Loss,* and for her generous commentary. It is an honour beyond measure to receive the first place award from an esteemed writer I so admire.

My appreciation is also extended to accomplished writers Kala Ramesh and Christina Sng, for their support during the pre-reading process.

Thank you to John Barlow, editor of Snapshot Press, for his encouraging note regarding an earlier version of the tanka portion of this manuscript.

I am indebted to Melissa Hassard and the Sable Books team for administering this contest, and for their dedication to the promotion of diverse voices. Thanks also to Daniel Krawiec for his design expertise.

About the Author

Debbie Strange makes poems, music, photographs, and art in Winnipeg, the heart of Canada. She has a deep reverence for nature, and feels most centred when exploring the wilds with her husband in their 1978 VW campervan. Debbie's creative passions help her to manage chronic illness, connecting her more closely to the world and to herself.

She is a member of the Manitoba Writers' Guild, as well as several tanka and haiku organizations. Her work has received multiple awards, and has been translated into 11 languages, anthologized, and published in 15 countries. Debbie was honoured to be a featured poet in the Tanka Society of America's journal, *Ribbons* (2019), the British short-form journal, *Presence* (2017), the Mann Library's Daily Haiku column (2016), and the United Haiku and Tanka Society's journal, *Cattails* (2014). The Haiku Foundation features a haiga gallery of Debbie's artworks which incorporate award-winning haiku and tanka.

A publication and awards archive, including hundreds of haiga, reviews of Debbie's two full-length books, *Three-Part Harmony: Tanka Verses* (Keibooks 2018), *Warp and Weft: Tanka Threads* (Keibooks 2015), and her haiku chapbook, *A Year Unfolding* (Folded Word 2017), may be accessed at debbiemstrange.blogspot.com.

Made in the USA
Las Vegas, NV
26 May 2021